THEN & NOW

BATTLE CREEK

In 1901, the Soldiers and Sailors Monument was dedicated at the intersection of Main Street, Division Street, and Marshall Street (now East Michigan Avenue) in front of the First Methodist Church and, eventually, the Battle Creek City Hall (as seen on the cover). The statue, entitled *Defense of the Flag*, was built by the Harrison Granite Company of Barre, Vermont, to commemorate Civil War veterans, in "Memory of our Heroes, 1861–1865." The area became known as Monument Square and was the center of the city's important civic events. The monument was moved to McCamly Park in 1966 as part of the construction of the Interstate 94 business route called the Penetrator. Frank Kellogg (see page 60) was instrumental in raising the $6,500 from veterans and citizens to pay for the memorial.

THEN & NOW

BATTLE CREEK

Martin Ashley and Kurt Thornton

ISBN 0-7385-3976-7

Published by Arcadia Publishing
Charleston SC, Chicago IL, Portsmouth NH, San Francisco CA

Printed in the United States of America

Library of Congress Catalog Card Number: 2005928477

For all general information contact Arcadia Publishing at:
Telephone 843-853-2070
Fax 843-853-0044
E-mail sales@arcadiapublishing.com
For customer service and orders:
Toll-Free 1-888-313-2665

Visit us on the Internet at http://www.arcadiapublishing.com

Shown is the construction of the Interstate 94 Penetrator. The $4 million project was designed to connect the Battle Creek central business district with the heavily traveled Interstate 94 highway between Chicago and Detroit. The photograph was taken looking north from the Columbia Avenue Bridge in 1965 (see page 6, present-day view). (Courtesy City of Battle Creek.)

Contents

ACKNOWLEDGMENTS

It is always a pleasure to have the opportunity to tell people about what an exciting place Battle Creek is. I particularly like to show my friends a historic site or relate an event that once happened here because I want them to share the exhilaration I feel when I discover something about the history of where I live. For these same reasons, I decided to write this book.

I would like to recognize the people, books, and institutions that helped with this project. These supporters and resources include my co-workers at Battle Creek Health System Surgical Services Team (you're still the best); the Battle Creek Historic District Commission Walking Tour brochures; *Battle Creek* (Images of America series); Diane Beckley; Michael Breitbach; Maura Brown, my editor at Arcadia Publishing; Mike Buckley; Mary Butler; Michael Gregory, *The Forgotten Years of Battle Creek*; the Historical Society of Battle Creek Archives; George Livingston; Jane Ratner; *Religious Heritage—Greater Battle Creek Churches: 1832–1976*; Susie Roeper; Junior and Frances Thornton; Kathy Thornton; the Willard Library Local History Collection; and Anna Wilson, my other editor at Arcadia Publishing.

Special mention goes to Ellsworth Willis Roberts, a lifelong resident of Battle Creek. During the period from 1931 to 1934, he compiled *Rambles with a Camera around Old Battle Creek*, 10 volumes of handwritten notebooks combined with over 1,500 photographs recording the city's history. The notebooks were donated to the Willard Library Local History Collection, where they have been transcribed and indexed. While he was trying to describe something about the pioneer past, he unintentionally recorded a view of Battle Creek in the early 20th century. Many of the photographs have been reproduced in this book.

Special thanks go to coauthor Martin Ashley. A lifelong resident of Battle Creek, he became interested in local history at a young age. He has been a member of the Board of Directors of the Historical Society of Battle Creek, a trustee and historian for Oak Hill Cemetery, and an ordained elder, deacon, and historian in the First Presbyterian Church.

To the readers, I hope the book sparks your awareness of this wonderful city. Thank you.

—Kurt Thornton

The Interstate 94 Penetrator followed a north–south valley created by glaciers during the Ice Age. The highway was opened to modern traffic in 1966. This present-day view was taken looking north from the Columbia Avenue Bridge (see page 4, early view).

INTRODUCTION

In March 1825, two men from a team sent to survey the Michigan Territory were left in camp (near present-day Bellevue) while the rest of their group, led by Col. John H. Mullett, went surveying. Two Americans Indians came into camp and requested food, as such sharing was customary in their society. After having eaten, they asked how many men were here and what the team was doing in this part of the wilderness. Upon receiving the answers, the Indians became agitated and ordered the two men to leave. A fight ensued, a gun was fired, and the Indians were tied up. Mullett's party returned and questioned the Indians, who were held overnight (to prevent them from immediately reporting back to their people) and released in the morning. The surveyors then broke camp and returned to Detroit. When it came time to assign a name to the creek near where the incident occurred, the surveyors thought it would be humorous to call it Battle Creek. In 1858, the village at the confluence of the Battle Creek River and the Kalamazoo River voted to call itself Battle Creek.

The location between the two rivers made Battle Creek an ideal place for water-powered mills. In 1835, Sands McCamly financed the digging of a one-and-a-quarter-mile-long millrace and the damming of the Kalamazoo River. With waterpower available, mills and other businesses thrived.

In 1845, the Michigan Central Railroad reached Battle Creek from Detroit. The town had the means to become a commercial and manufacturing center. New industry sprang up, including the Nichols and Shepard Company, builders of threshing machines that eventually reached every corner of the globe.

The possibility of worldwide connections was also noticed by some religious organizations. In 1855, the Seventh-Day Adventists moved their printing company, the Review and Herald, from Rochester, New York, to Battle Creek. The founder of the Adventist church, Ellen White, had the headquarters of the church moved here also, along with an orphanage, schools, and a health center, the Battle Creek Sanitarium. Based on White's clean biological living teachings, the sanitarium under the direction of Dr. John Harvey Kellogg became an institution respected around the world. Kellogg not only practiced medicine, he also wrote 50 books, designed surgical equipment, made the first peanut butter, personally invented 80 different grain and nut products, and, with his brother Will Keith Kellogg, co-invented flaked cereal.

The doctor was not interested in commercializing his inventions, but his brother thought it was bad business to let other people make money off of his brother's invention. In 1906, W. K. Kellogg began producing cereal for public sale, eventually making his company the largest cereal manufacturer in the world. Along with C. W. Post, he made Battle Creek "the Cereal City."

Change is what history is all about. Prior to the invention of photography, artwork and memory were the only way to record events. Today, there are film and tape and digital, still, and moving pictures. All can provide a window into another time.

Books in Arcadia Publishing's Then & Now series offer an interesting way to remember changes that have taken place in a community. The past, even the recent past, tends to get hazy, and a photograph taken years ago can serve as a clear reminder of a business, home, or landmark from the past. This volume on Battle Creek history will spark memories, as the camera has returned to the old locations and has captured the views of today.

The authors believe that they have selected an interesting variety of photographs and only wish that they could have covered the city's entire heritage. Further information on Battle Creek history is available from Heritage Battle Creek, (269) 965-2613, and Willard Library's Local History Collection, (269) 968-8166.

Change is constant. Even from decade to decade, the march of time is evident. The earlier photograph (left) was taken looking southeast on McCamly Street from State Street in the early 1980s. The structure being demolished is the Post Building. That building was opened in 1901 by C. W. Post as a state-of-the-art office-retail facility and was joined by an over-the-road bridge to the Post Tavern Hotel, on the southwest corner of West Michigan Avenue and McCamly Street. The building on the left was constructed in 1928 on the site of the 1896 Presbyterian church as a J. C. Penney store. Later, it became Coles Clothing Store and then a hairstyling school. Today, it houses a dance club. The more recent picture shows construction work being done on Michigan Avenue. (Unless otherwise noted, all photographs are courtesy of Kurt Thornton; upper photograph courtesy City of Battle Creek.)

Chapter 1
BUSINESS, PARKS, AND STREET SCENES

This chapter contains a very general selection of scenes. Because change happens everywhere, an effort was made to include many areas of the city of Battle Creek. Many of the very old parts of the city were gone before photography was available, but a large treasury of pictures from the late 1800s to the present is preserved at the Willard Library, the Historical Society of Battle Creek, and in many private collections. This late-1800s photograph was taken looking east from the McCamly Street Bridge over the Battle Creek River. The Michigan Central train station (see page 43), now the restaurant Clara's on the River, is in the center. The American Steam Pump factory, with the flag flying, is on the right. The spire of St. Thomas Episcopal Church rises over the station's roof. (Courtesy Frances Thornton Collection.)

In 1933, James H. Brown (1859–1938) began constructing a stone tower, or cairn, in Monument Park near the northeast corner of Division Street and Jackson Street. The early view, taken looking northwest from the corner of Jackson Street and South Avenue, shows the stones waiting to be put in place. Brown was the first person in the United States to organize "conducted automobile tours." While leading the tours, he gathered stones from historic sites around the country to use in the tower. More than stones are included in the structure—among the artifacts are a wheel from the Duplex Printing Company's first printing press, a tablet made from metal retrieved from the battleship *Maine*, and a German army helmet from World War I. The tower now welcomes people to downtown Battle Creek from behind the fountain and entrance to the city in Monument Park. (Upper photograph courtesy E. W. Roberts Collection of Willard Library.)

The block from the corner of Jackson Street and East Michigan Avenue teems with business in the early 1930s. The bell tower of the First Baptist Church rises in the distance of this photograph, taken looking northwest from the corner of Jackson Street and East Michigan Avenue. By the 1960s, the whole block was owned by Star Appliances, which had a showroom and warehouses. By September 1999, the entire block had been demolished and the section of South Avenue between Jackson Street and Michigan Avenue had been removed to make a larger Monument Park. The statue of C. W. Post, designed by J. Gelert and erected by the citizens of Battle Creek in 1916, was moved to the corner facing the Post Cereal plant, making room for an education area featuring a 12-foot statue of Sojourner Truth by Tina Allen. (Lower photograph courtesy E. W. Roberts Collection of Willard Library.)

The 1960s photograph (above) was taken looking southwest from the corner of East Michigan Avenue and Division Street. The Bromberg Block (left) was the site of a jewelry store built by Henry Bromberg in 1911. The Bell Telephone building (right) was erected in the 1920s. The First Baptist Church education building (far right) was constructed in 1958. In November 1970, the Bromberg Block was demolished and replaced by an addition to the Michigan Bell Telephone Company. The telephone company building that faced Michigan Avenue was torn down in the 1990s; a four-story section covered with decorative features remains. (Upper photograph courtesy Willard Library.)

This post office building was designed in the Beaux-Arts style by Detroit architect Albert Kahn and completed in May 1907, facing East Michigan Avenue. It was enlarged in 1931 and remained in use until 1968, when the post office moved to its new home on McCamly Street. The 1960s photograph, taken from the corner of State and Division Streets, shows the facility's State Street loading dock. From 1968 to 1979, the building sat empty. It was then renovated into the hall of justice to house the circuit and district courts and city and county offices. After a new justice complex was opened in the 1990s, the building became Commerce Pointe, with offices for city, business, nonprofit agencies, the visitors' bureau, and the Battle Creek Chamber of Commerce. (Lower photograph courtesy Willard Library.)

The Masonic Temple, at 133 East Michigan Avenue, was dedicated in 1914. Designed by Grand Rapids architects Osgood and Osgood, the $85,000 five-story building was built of Wadsworth paving brick and was trimmed in white terra cotta. It contains a large auditorium-ballroom, lodge rooms, dining rooms, and ceremonial spaces. Today, it continues to function as a center for area fraternal orders. The boulder and plaque in front of the structure commemorates Battle Creek's first log cabin, built by Jonathan Guernsey in 1831. (Upper photograph courtesy Frances Thornton Collection.)

In the early 1920s, local architect A. B. Chanel designed an automobile dealership and garage for Dudley Motors Sales Company. In April 1937, Robert H. Holmes Inc. took over the Ford dealership at the site, at 151 East Michigan Avenue on the northwest corner of East Michigan Avenue and Jackson Street. The building was demolished in the 1980s, and the Calhoun County Justice and Correctional Center was opened on the site in the 1990s. The building currently contains the circuit court, district courts, and the county jail. (Lower photograph courtesy Willard Library.)

The four-story Potter House was built in 1881 at a cost of $20,000. Located at 36–40 Main Street, the hotel was designed by Chicago architect Edward Bowman with the upper floors laid out in French flats, long narrow apartments built around a skylighted central atrium. The 1930s view was taken looking southeast from the corner of Main Street (now East Michigan Avenue) and Monroe Street. The Potter Block was rehabilitated in 1984 by local architect Randy Case to house his architectural firm. (Upper photograph courtesy E. W. Roberts Collection of Willard Library.)

The M. McCamly building, on East Michigan Avenue, was constructed over the millrace in the early 1900s. It housed retail businesses (among them a barbershop, drugstore, and hat blocking shop) on the lower level, which ran back along Monroe Street. It was demolished in the late 1980s as part of the W. K. Kellogg Foundation's $80 million downtown redevelopment, which included a new headquarters building and park. On August 24, 1991, Millrace Park was dedicated to commemorate city founder Sands McCamly's millrace (see page 48). The waterfall runs throughout the summer and features sculptured panels, created by artist Tim Woodman, depicting the history of the waterway. The 1901 Battle Creek Gas Company building (left), at 26 East Michigan Avenue,

was designed by Jackson architect E. C. Grosvenor. In 1965, the gas company moved its offices and Ermisch Travel purchased the building. (Lower photograph courtesy Willard Library.)

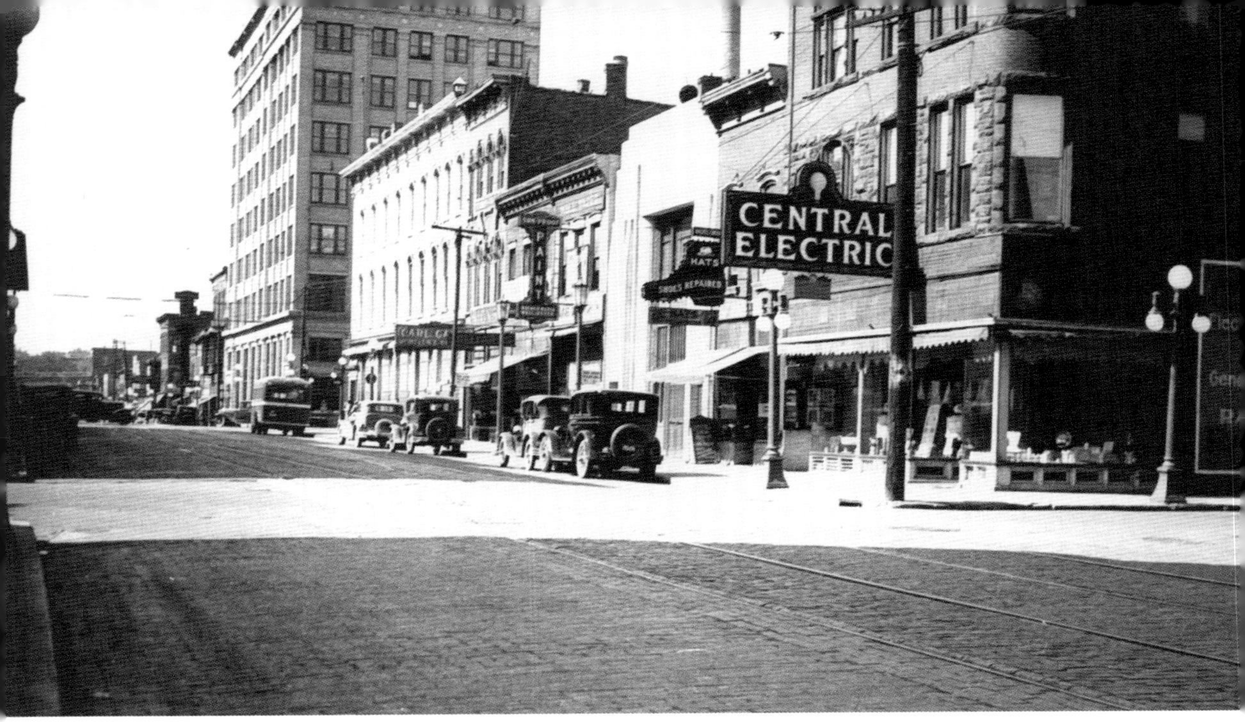

The American-style eight-story City Bank Building (left) was designed by Jackson-Casse Engineering of Chicago and opened in 1915. In 1941, it became Michigan National Bank. It was demolished in the early 1990s and replaced by a two-story structure. The McCamly Plaza Hotel can be seen in the distance of this view of Jefferson Street (now Capital Avenue Northeast), which was taken looking southwest from State Street. The John terAvest Agency renovated its building and remains as the only surviving structure on the block. Calhoun Federal Savings built the bank (right), and it became Great Lakes Federal Savings before closing in the late 1990s. (Upper photograph courtesy E. W. Roberts Collection of Willard Library.)

In 1956, People's Savings and Loan Association renovated 2–4 West Michigan Avenue into a modern banking facility by sheathing the old building with grey marble. This was the site of Battle Creek's first hotel, the Battle Creek House, which opened in 1836. The hotel burned in 1866; reputedly the fire was set by temperance fanatics who opposed the selling of alcoholic spirits at the tavern. The Thomas Block was built in 1890; a portion of it (left) can still be seen in the early photograph. People's Savings and Loan Association went out of business in the 1980s; the building is now called Two West Michigan. (Lower photograph courtesy Willard Library.)

The Old National Bank was housed in the 1860s Whitcomb Block. The bank first occupied the building in September 1865. The early-1900s photograph shows the northeast corner of Jefferson Street (now Capital Avenue Northeast) and Main Street (now East Michigan Avenue). These buildings had all been demolished by 1989. The W. K. Kellogg Foundation opened its building in 1991 as part of an $80 million downtown redevelopment. The facility is designed to house a staff of 300 people. The foundation, one of the largest philanthropic organizations in the country, celebrated its 75th anniversary in 2005. (Upper photograph courtesy Frances Thornton Collection.)

In 1904, Peter Zang built the three-story Zang Block on the southeast corner of Jefferson Street (now Capital Avenue Northeast) and State Street. Next to it was the Boos-McKinstry Block, built in 1907. It was used as a barbershop, a billiard parlor, and a Piggly Wiggly grocery store from 1922 to 1940. In the 1980s, it housed Input One, a bar and dance club. The streets (foreground) are being repaired after the parking structure over the Battle Creek River was removed. Both the Zang and the Boos-McKinstry Blocks were demolished in 1988 to make way for the W. K. Kellogg Foundation building.

The Hamblin Opera House, city hall (built in 1867), and the tower of the Congregational-Presbyterian church can be seen in the 1869 photograph of Main Street (now West Michigan Avenue), taken looking southwest from the intersection of Jefferson Street (now Capital Avenue Northeast). The opera house was opened in 1868 at a cost of $40,000. The second-floor auditorium, which could hold 1,200 people, was the cultural center of the city until the Post Theatre opened in 1902. The opera house then became a movie theater and, in 1921, Toellers clothing store. Still standing, it is currently a restaurant. Today, the Heritage Tower resides on the site of the old city hall. Designed by the Chicago firm of Weary and Alford, the 20-story tower is the tallest in Battle Creek. The building was originally the Old Merchants National Bank, opened on August 15, 1931. The banking room's interior decorations are considered to be among the finest examples of Art Deco design in southwest Michigan. (Upper photograph courtesy Historical Society of Battle Creek.)

These three photographs were taken from near the corner of McCamly Street, looking southeast along West Michigan Avenue. The lower photograph dates from around 1965. The two more recent photographs show the $2 million pedestrian Michigan Mall, dedicated in 1975 and removed in the late 1990s, and the annual Longest Breakfast Table in the World cereal festival of 2005. (Lower photograph courtesy City of Battle Creek; middle photograph courtesy Frances Thornton Collection.)

The Hammond Block was built at 30 West Michigan Avenue on the central downtown block in 1893 by local businessman Nicholas Hammond. It was sold in 1950 to a chain of discount stores called McLellan's, who remodeled the exterior of the building but retained the building's name, Hammond, at the top of the storefront (as seen in the *c.* 1950s view to the left). The building has been home to many businesses but is currently vacant. The roofs of Battle Creek Central High School and W. K. Kellogg Auditorium can be seen in the distance. (Photographs courtesy Willard Library.)

These three photographs were taken from the south side of West Michigan Avenue, looking toward the northeast corner of McCamly Street. The *c.* 1900 photograph (below) shows the Presbyterian church that occupied the site from 1883 to 1928. In 1928, the church was replaced by a J. C. Penney store. The structure is now home to a financial advisory company, silkscreen printers, and a dance club. (Lower photograph courtesy Frances Thornton Collection; middle photograph courtesy E. W. Roberts Collection of Willard Library.)

In 1931, the Central National Bank built an 18-story office building on the northwest corner of West Michigan Avenue and McCamly Street. The Indiana limestone–clad building was designed by Chicago architects Holabird and Root. In 1971, it was named Wolverine Tower and, in 1984, the Transamerica Building. Today, it is called the Battle Creek Tower. The Post Tavern Hotel stands across the street, with the pedestrian bridge connecting it to the Post Building (left). Both photographs were taken looking south from the corner of State and McCamly Streets. (Upper photograph courtesy Frances Thornton Collection.)

On October 21, 1941, the Michigan Theatre opened its doors at 75 West Michigan Avenue. The 1950s photograph shows children waiting in line for the weekly Kiddies Morning Show held each Saturday. The Post Tavern Hotel (left) was demolished in the early 1960s, and the movie theater was torn down in October 1984. The site is now a small park featuring a horse sculpture presented to the city by the president of the Transamerica Insurance Company. The Fifth Third Bank building is the modern, glass-clad structure on the corner. (Lower photograph courtesy Willard Library.)

On September 19, 1930, the Montgomery Ward store opened at 110 West Michigan Avenue next to Louis Grill, an old streetcar converted to a restaurant. The area is teeming with business in the 1930s photograph, taken from the corner of Carlisle Street looking at the north side of West Michigan Avenue. Most of the buildings were demolished in 1988 and replaced by a municipal parking lot. The $8 million West Michigan Avenue Center parking structure was completed in 1997. (Upper photograph courtesy E. W. Roberts Collection of Willard Library.)

The early view of the south side of West Michigan Avenue was taken looking east from Carlisle Street. On the corner is the three-story Mapes Hotel, constructed in 1923. In 1933, the building at 119–121 West Michigan Avenue became the Anson Hotel, which closed in 1997. The building next to the hotel at 115–117 West Michigan Avenue is the Alex Ratti Store. These two buildings, along with a structure on Carlisle Street, are being developed into residential living space called Riverfront Condominiums. The hope is that the downtown can be revitalized by having more people live and work in the central business district. (Lower photograph courtesy E. W. Roberts Collection of Willard Library.)

The *c.* 1980 view of the southwest corner of West Michigan Avenue and Carlisle Street shows the Hebble Funeral Home, built by Andrew Hebble in 1914, with a 1923 addition. The brick building with flat Gothic arches over the windows was built above the Battle Creek River by contractor A. S. Weddle. The funeral home moved from this site in 1987. All the buildings in this photograph were demolished and the river views opened up when Kellogg's Cereal City U.S.A. was built. (Upper photograph courtesy City of Battle Creek.)

Located on the former site of city founder Sands McCamly's house, the 1890 Nichols Memorial Hospital with a 1901 addition is pictured in the 1930s. The hospital moved and was renamed Community Hospital on September 12, 1938. These buildings were torn down and replaced by Summit Pointe. The fieldstone *Moon Journal* newspaper building was built in 1915 and became part of the *Enquirer and News* until it was demolished in the late 1990s. (Lower photograph courtesy E. W. Roberts Collection of Willard Library.)

The house on the southeast corner of Van Buren and Tompkins Streets was built by Michael Neale, who started a local shoe business in 1850. The Neale house and the other elegant homes in the 1930s photograph were replaced in 1952 by the white Indiana limestone *Enquirer and News* building. (Upper photograph courtesy E. W. Roberts Collection of Willard Library.)

The Dairy Queen ice-cream store on Gould Street is being demolished in this 1983 photograph taken looking east from McCamly Park. The Burnham Brook Center (named after a now underground stream) was opened in 1985 as a senior citizen recreation center, replacing the Valentine Center in Irving Park. It contains exercise areas, a swimming pool, a woodworking shop, arts and crafts areas, a small library, and a restaurant. (Lower photograph courtesy Willard Library.)

McCamly Park and the steeple of the 1878 Seventh-Day Adventist Dime Tabernacle are seen in the *c.* 1900 photograph, taken looking west on West Michigan Avenue from the corner of Gould Street. The church's title reflects the way its construction was achieved; Seventh-Day Adventists worldwide were asked to donate one dime per week until the $26,000 needed to erect the tabernacle was collected. The structure burned on January 7, 1922. It was replaced in 1926 by a new tabernacle, designed by local architect A. B. Chanel. The bank building on the corner and the tabernacle are shown in the 1950s photograph. (Upper photograph courtesy Frances Thornton Collection; lower photograph courtesy Willard Library.)

The Seventh-Day Adventist printing plant, the Review and Herald Publishing Company, burned on December 30, 1902. Its site on the southeast corner of West Michigan and Washington Avenues is shown in the 1930s, occupied by the 1907 Allen Block. The building housed the West End Hotel and later the McCamly Park Hotel, which closed in 1965. It is currently the local office of Rep. John Schwarz. (Lower photograph courtesy E. W. Roberts Collection of Willard Library.)

In 1986, the Kellogg Company corporate headquarters on McCamly Street was completed at a cost of $70 million. Hellmuth, Obata, and Kassabaum designed the five-story, 300,000-square-foot facility. At the dedication, company president William LaMothe said that the headquarters "represents the company's commitment to the people of the community. Placed in the central business district, it is a living symbol of a company dedicated to its Battle Creek heritage." It is constructed over the former Kalamazoo River bed, and the back lawn is the site of the original confluence of the Battle Creek and Kalamazoo Rivers.

In 1900, Sherman Manufacturing built a four-story factory on the northwest corner of Jackson and Barney Streets to produce plumbing fixtures. When the Kalamazoo River Diversion Project was finished in 1962, the small footbridge replaced the former Barney Street Bridge. The factory was demolished to make way for Kellogg's Cereal City U.S.A., at 171 West Michigan Avenue. The tourist attraction opened in 1998 and was partially funded by Kellogg Company retirees. It houses exhibits that tell the story of the cereal industry through interactive displays, as well as a simulated cereal production line. (Lower photograph courtesy City of Battle Creek.)

Because of its location at the confluence of the Battle Creek and Kalamazoo Rivers, the city has been plagued with floods since its inception. The early picture shows the Michigan Central bridge over the Kalamazoo River during the March 1947 flood. Considered one of the area's worst, the flood sparked the local and national governments to begin the $7 million Kalamazoo River Diversion Project. In 1981, the railroad lines in the city were combined, eliminating the need for the bridge. In 1987, the bridge was remodeled for pedestrians use as part of the 11-mile Linear Park system that runs throughout the city. (Upper photograph courtesy Willard Library.)

The construction of the "cement river," the Kalamazoo River Diversion Project, is shown in a November 1960 view, looking south toward the Kalamazoo River Dam from the Fountain Street Bridge. The $7 million project moved the Kalamazoo and Battle Creek River confluence west of the central business district and straightened the crooked river west of the city to lessen chances of its flooding. Much of the lower-income residential area known as the Flats or the Bottoms was demolished as part of urban renewal. (Lower photograph courtesy Frances Thornton Collection.)

The Sullivan Barn, at 49 South Cass Street, was originally used to house horses and milk wagons for the Sullivan Dairy. It was designed by E. W. Arnold, who also designed Battle Creek City Hall. Horses were stabled in the lower part, and hay was stored in the upper part. After World War II, the horses were eliminated and milk trucks were stored there. The dairy was sold to a Detroit firm in 1969, and the barn remained empty, as shown in the 1980s photograph. In 2002, the building was remodeled for office space by local architectural firm Architects Incorporated PC and named Historic Sullivan Barn. (Upper photograph courtesy City of Battle Creek.)

On October 10, 1905, the six-story Ward Building opened at 23 Jefferson Street (now Capital Avenue Northeast). It was the first completely fireproof steel-and-concrete building between Detroit and Chicago. The top floor contained a men's lounge, a gymnasium, and an auditorium-ballroom used by the Athelston Club, a social group. In 1931, the club relocated to the Old Merchant National Bank Building to avoid the smoke and noise from the Michigan Central Railroad next door. The building was demolished in 1987, and the site became Friendship Park. (Lower photograph courtesy City of Battle Creek.)

This photograph of the 1904 flood was taken on Jefferson Street (now Capital Avenue Northeast), looking north from the Battle Creek River Bridge. The Charles Willard Library is under construction on the left. The 1879 St. Philip Catholic Church spire rises in the center. The American Steam Pump Company stands on the right. The St. Thomas Episcopal Church spire can be seen in both photographs. The factory was demolished in the 1960s, but the building's foundation can still be seen in the wall around the church parking lot. (Upper photograph courtesy Frances Thornton Collection.)

The Michigan Central train station, at 44 North McCamly Street, was opened on June 27, 1888. The Detroit firm of Rogers and McFarland designed the Romanesque-style structure, which is shown in the 1980s with signs of neglect and a fire. In the 1960s, the city built a parking structure over the Battle Creek River that blocked the view of the water. The parking deck was removed in the mid-1980s, and the Linear Park replaced the railroad tracks after a new train and bus station opened on South McCamly Street. Today, the former railway station is a restaurant, Clara's on the River, with Friendship Park in the foreground. (Lower photograph courtesy City of Battle Creek.)

The house in the center of the 1880s photograph was owned by John Champion. The view is looking northeast from the intersection of State Street and McCamly Street. Champion started one brickyard on the shore of Goguac Lake and, later, another brickyard at the northwest corner of Champion and West Streets. The house originally faced Water Street, which was eventually acquired by the Michigan Central Railroad and used as the bed for its tracks. The wooden gates (right) were used to keep not only residents but also livestock from wandering onto the tracks. W. K. Kellogg Auditorium and Junior High School is visible in the present-day photograph. The $700,000 school was a gift to the city from W. K. Kellogg in 1933. The International-style building was designed by Detroit architect Albert Kahn. The Battle Creek River is in the foreground. (Upper photograph courtesy Frances Thornton Collection.)

The Kneip Market stands on the site that eventually became that of the McCamly Plaza Hotel. The December 8, 1937, view was taken from the corner of Jackson Street looking south on Capital Avenue Southwest. The McCamly Plaza Hotel, originally called the Stouffer Hotel, opened in 1981 as part of the $26 million McCamly Square-Kellogg Center sports arena-exhibition hall. The 15-story, 248-room hotel features a 600-seat ballroom, two restaurants, and an indoor pool. (Lower photograph courtesy Frances Thornton Collection.)

The LaSalle Hotel, at 45–47 Capital Avenue Southwest, was built in 1927. The Hi-Lo Club opened as a bar and restaurant in 1933. There, pop singer Del Shannon first performed his hit "Runaway" in 1961. In 1952, the hotel was purchased by Phillip Gilbert, who changed the name to the Gilbert Hotel. The hotel was closed in 1978 and demolished in 1984. A state historical marker commemorating Del Shannon was erected on the site of the Hi-Lo Club, on the northeast corner of Capital Avenue Southwest and Hamblin Avenue. The base of the marker is designed to look like a record. (Upper photograph courtesy Willard Library.)

In the 1930s view, looking west on Jackson Street near the intersection of Capital Avenue Southwest, are, from left to right, the Post Tavern Hotel, the Bijou Theatre (a movie and vaudeville venue, demolished in 1984), the Kewpie Hamburg stand, the No. 1 Fire Station, and the Old Merchant Bank Building. In the 1950s, the Karmel Korn Shop occupied the store at the Jackson Street entrance to the bank's arcade, and the aroma was sweet. In the present-day view are, from left to right, the Fifth Third Bank, Western Michigan University Kendall Center (at 50 West Jackson), Battle Creek Community Foundation (at 34 West Jackson), and the back entrance to Heritage Tower. (Lower photograph courtesy E. W. Roberts Collection of Willard Library.)

In 1835, Sands McCamly built a one-and-a-quarter-mile-long millrace between the Kalamazoo and the Battle Creek Rivers. The 40-foot-wide canal provided enough waterpower for the village's mills and factories, which at the height consisted of 18 businesses. The 1950s view of the waterway was taken looking west from Beacon Street between Fountain and Jackson Streets. During the Kalamazoo River Diversion Project, the millrace was removed and filled in. The entrance driveway to the W. K. Kellogg Institute for Food and Nutrition on Jackson Street follows the same path as the former millrace. (Upper photograph courtesy Willard Library.)

The unusual flatiron (triangular) building was constructed in 1890 along Monroe Street. It was built behind the Binder meat company building at 34 East Michigan Avenue as a slaughterhouse. Animals for the wholesale meat business were raised to the top floor through a central atrium. The carcasses then were lowered floor by floor to be butchered by each floor's area of expertise. The 1857 house (right) faced Monroe Street and the millrace. It was owned by Dr. DeWitt Clinton Addington, a local physician and real estate investor. The house was demolished in the 1930s. (Lower photograph courtesy E. W. Roberts Collection of Willard Library.)

This section of Irving Park includes the bridge over the Spring Lake stream and Walter Avenue going uphill. The 1919 photograph shows the park under construction. A 1930s photograph shows the rustic 1928 stone bridge. The present-day photograph reveals what remains of the buried sandstone wall, with the stream rerouted underground. (Upper photograph courtesy Frances Thornton Collection; middle photograph courtesy E. W. Roberts Collection of Willard Library.)

Dedicated in 1924, Irving Park was a gift to the city by Battle Creek businessman Irving Stone. The park included streams, ponds, rock gardens with stone grottos, and a 400-year-old white oak tree, all developed from a swampy area on the city's north side. Pictured in the 1930s, this pond was between the Battle Creek Sanitarium (now the Hart, Dole, and Inouye Federal Center) and the Youth Building. It was drained and replaced in 1961 by C. W. Post Field, part of Battle Creek Central High School's athletic complex. (Lower photograph courtesy E. W. Roberts Collection of Willard Library.)

This 1930s photograph was taken looking southeast on North Avenue from the intersection of Calhoun Street. From left to right are the Trumbull Service Station, at 54 Calhoun Street, the home of George Willard, and other houses. Most of the homes were either demolished or converted to apartments or businesses. Meyer's Toy World, at 72 North Avenue, continues to be a family-owned business. (Upper photograph courtesy E. W. Roberts Collection of Willard Library.)

Sumner Bush, vice president and general manager of the Advance Thresher Company, built this home on Maple Street (now Capital Avenue Northeast) in 1907. It was later used as Maple Street Hospital and then remodeled as the YMCA in 1940. The earlier photograph shows the 1952 gymnasium addition. In 1971, the house was demolished to make way for the $2.7 million Y Center. In 1973, the old gym (still visible) was incorporated into the new facility. The building was remodeled again in 2003. (Lower photograph courtesy City of Battle Creek.)

Dr. Arthur Kimball built the Queen Anne–style residence at 196 Maple Street (now Capital Avenue) in 1886. The house on the right was built in 1884 for Dr. John H. Penniman, a dentist. Kimball's son, Dr. Arthur S. Kimball, acquired 196 Maple Street in 1894 and became one of Battle Creek's most influential physicians. He worked with Dr. John Harvey Kellogg to establish open-air schools, in which ailing children were invigorated with a regimen of fresh air, diet, and exercise. He also helped found the area tuberculosis hospital. The family donated the house to the Junior League after the third generation of Kimball doctors, Arthur S. Kimball Jr., passed away in 1966. The Junior League renovated the home and donated it to the Historical Society of Battle Creek, which continues to operate it as the Kimball House Museum, a Victorian house museum with special displays featuring local history. The building on the right is the Y Center. (Upper photograph courtesy Frances Thornton Collection.)

In 1949, local architect A. B. Chanel designed the Colonial-style Christian Reformed Church at 265 Emmett Street. The building was donated to the Battle Creek Civic Art Center in 1964, in part by George C. McKay. In 1974 and 1979, additions were constructed, enlarging the gallery space and classroom areas. The roofline of the old church can still be seen. The Battle Creek Civic Art Center possesses one of the state's largest collections of Michigan resident artwork. (Lower photograph courtesy Willard Library.)

Pioneer Ezra Convis founded the community of Verona in the mid-1800s as a rival to Battle Creek, a few miles downriver. He built a dam on the Battle Creek River and created a business district. His dream of a city ended when he died as a result of a sleighing accident. The 1947 photograph was taken from the corner of Maple Grove Avenue, looking north on Capital Avenue Northeast. The half-timbered building (center) became Speed's of Verona, part of a popular chain of local restaurants; it burned in the late 1990s. Most of the buildings on the east side of the street have been demolished. (Upper photograph courtesy Carol Bennett Collection.)

Ezra Convis built the Verona Dam as a source of power for what he hoped would be a thriving manufacturing area. After his death, the downtown Battle Creek mills became the predominant industrial area. During its existence, the dam has powered only two mills: one near the corner of Wagner Drive and Emmett Street, and the mill pictured here in the 1920s. The mills were demolished in the 1940s, leaving only the dam. The city's Linear Park extended walkways and observation platforms to the dam in the 1990s. These views are looking west from the east side of the Battle Creek River. (Lower photograph courtesy Carol Bennett Collection.)

In 1924, the Grand Trunk Railroad built this roundhouse on the south side of Emmett Street near the Grand Trunk switching yards. The roundhouse replaced an outdated 1884 building nearer downtown. The structure could accommodate 45 steam engines at one time for maintenance, as shown in the 1930s photograph. A fire destroyed part of the building in the early 1970s. The later view shows the roof collapsed and foliage growing in the debris; shortly after the photograph was taken, the building was demolished. (Upper photograph courtesy Willard Library.)

W. K. Kellogg opened the Kellogg's Toasted Corn Flake factory on Porter Street in January 1908. The building was designed by Chicago architect M. J. Morehouse. Over the years, many additions were made to the factory, which became the largest producer of breakfast cereal in the world. The *c.* 1980 photograph shows the construction of an employee cafeteria. As the business climate changed, so did the ability to produce cereal cost-effectively in Battle Creek. The highly automated, state-of-the-art Building One factory was constructed behind this building, and the factory facing Porter Street was demolished. (Lower photograph courtesy City of Battle Creek.)

Oak Hill Cemetery was established in 1844 on the south side of Battle Creek. As the city expanded, the older cemeteries located at Quaker Park (on Fremont Street) and Washington Avenue (now the site of the Hart, Dole and Inouye Federal Center) were moved to the property at 255 South Avenue. Many famous Battle Creek residents, including W. K. Kellogg, Dr. John Harvey Kellogg, C. W. Post, Sojourner Truth, and Ellen and James White, are buried at the 75-acre site. The *c.* 1916 photograph shows the construction of the tomb of local entrepreneur Frank Kellogg. Kellogg's monument is the tallest in the cemetery. The present-day photograph shows C. W. Post's mausoleum (right). (Upper photograph courtesy Frances Thornton Collection.)

Allen H. Penniman built Penniman's Castle, the fieldstone house at 443 Main Street, for his wife, Fayette Penniman, in 1905. No expense was spared in the design of materials. A large, three-story central rotunda was open to the third-floor ballroom. The family moved to California in 1910. The house was remodeled in 1914, with English-style gables replacing the towers on the third floor. After a 1941 fire destroyed the ballroom, a new second-story flat roof was built. In the 1960s, Roland Smith purchased the home and restored much of its grandeur. The current owner, who acquired it in 1994, has reopened the rotunda on the second floor and continues the restoration. (Lower photograph courtesy Martin Ashley Collection; upper photograph courtesy Frances Thornton Collection.)

This house, located on Riverside Drive near the southeast corner of Territorial Road, is considered the oldest brick residence in Battle Creek. Pictured in the 1930s, it was built in 1852 as the home of Warren B. Shepard, the city's first schoolteacher. Shepard lived there until his death on December 17, 1875. In 1996, the Western Michigan Archeological Field School conducted a dig at the site and unearthed several thousand artifacts and clues to former outbuilding foundations. Today, the house is owned by the Historical Society of Battle Creek. (Upper photograph courtesy E. W. Roberts Collection of Willard Library.)

This full-service gas station was opened in 1929 at the northeast corner of Capital Avenue Southwest and Burnham Street. Charles Taylor owned the building, which was designed by his son, Howard Taylor. The Taylors were especially proud of their "grease palace," and its state-of-the-art automobile bays with built-in oil pits. The building, currently called Stanleys, appears to be vacant. (Lower photograph courtesy Martin Ashley Collection.)

This shopping complex was built in the 1930s on the southwest corner of Capital Avenue Southwest and Bidwell Street. It had a Kroger grocery store, a Rexall pharmacy, and a Shell gas station on the corner. During the 1940s, Lally's Drug Store was a popular place for teenagers to go. Over the years, an S&H Green Stamp store, the Subvilla Pizza Parlor, and a Ben Franklin store have occupied parts of the building. (Upper photograph courtesy Willard Library.)

The 1930s photograph shows the Lakeview business district on the northeast corner of Capital Avenue Southwest and Richards Street. Streetcar tracks ran along the west side of Capital Avenue, giving the area its distinct parking design. In the 1960s, these buildings were home to Security National Bank's Lakeview Branch, Alexander Pharmacy, the Speed's restaurant, and other varied businesses. (Lower photograph courtesy Willard Library.)

Steedman's was located on the southwest corner of Columbia Avenue and Capital Avenue Southwest. The store was built in 1918 by Charles Steedman, using lumber salvaged from Camp Custer army barracks. In 1946, the business was purchased by Clem Munger. From 1953 to 1967, the store held a popular Halloween party. The business closed in 1970. A Shell gas station with a food mart now occupies the corner. (Upper photograph courtesy Martin Ashley Collection.)

Columbia Plaza, Battle Creek's first "one-stop shopping center," opened in October 1958 on the west side of 20th Street between Columbia Avenue and Territorial Road. The plaza consisted of 15 individual stores, as shown in the 1960s photograph, taken looking south from the north side of the parking lot. Over the years, the plaza has been remodeled to its present mansard-style roof. This area was once part of the Battle Creek Sanitarium Farms, which produced vegetables and dairy products for the institution. The dairy barn, still located north of the plaza, houses an automotive parts store. (Lower photograph courtesy Frances Thornton Collection.)

Memorial Day 1947 marked the opening of the Elbert Ashley Florist on the southwest corner of Columbia Avenue and Helmer Road. The three greenhouse buildings had been dismantled and moved from the Walter Cole Florist on Wendell Street. The building on the corner in the 1950s photograph was built by Elbert Ashley and his son, Karl Ashley. The business closed in 1979. A strip mall now occupies the corner. (Upper photograph courtesy Martin Ashley Collection.)

Construction on the $40 million Lakeview Square Mall got under way on the northeast corner of Beckley Road and Riverside Drive *c.* 1982. Located south of Interstate 94 between Riverside Drive and the Penetrator (M-66), the 650,000-square-foot building was designed by Forbes-Cohen Development to house 112 stores. The mall opened on August 3, 1983, and featured sculpture by Michigan artists and the first planned picnic and food court. Its opening marked a move of the retail shopping area to the city's south side. (Lower photograph courtesy City of Battle Creek.)

On September 24, 1924, the Battle Creek Chamber of Commerce convinced the City of Battle Creek to lease the Garret Wells farm and create an airport. In 1928, W. K. Kellogg bought the original 100 acres, leased 50 more, and constructed an airplane hangar on Territorial Road. The 1930s photograph was taken looking west from the intersection of Helmer and Territorial Roads. Farms can be seen in the background. Territorial Road is now closed to through traffic, and a new $5 million control tower stands near the old Kellogg Hanger, by Skanska Construction Company. (Upper photograph courtesy Willard Library.)

After World War II, the Kellogg Airfield was returned to civilian use. The airport was certified a Class 5 field, capable of handling the largest land-based aircraft. In 1955, North Central Airlines began providing regularly scheduled service, and in 1958, this terminal and administration building at 237 North Helmer were opened. In the 1990s, Western Michigan University School of Aviation began classes at Kellogg Airport. New classrooms and mechanical buildings, designed by architects Tower, Pinkster, and Titus Associates, were opened in 1996. The school is now known as Western Michigan University College of Aviation. (Lower photograph courtesy Willard Library.)

Leila Y. Post Montgomery, C. W. Post's widow, donated the 72-acre former Battle Creek Country Club on West Michigan Avenue to the city in 1922 for development into an arboretum. The plan was to plant at least one of every type of tree that can thrive in Michigan soil. In 1931, local architect A. B. Chanel designed the Kingman Museum of Natural History, shown in the 1950s photograph. The museum was a gift of Emma Kingman to the Battle Creek public schools, in memory of her husband, Sen. A. C. Kingman, who served as an attorney for Nichols and Shepard Threshing Machine Company for 20 years. It was the first museum owned and operated by a public school system in the United States. The arboretum has been refurbished with more plantings, paved paths, a peace labyrinth, and a children's garden (see page 89). The museum has recently reopened after being closed by the public school system because of budgetary constraints. (Upper photograph courtesy Frances Thornton Collection.)

In 1838, Nathaniel Barney opened his third inn and stagecoach stop west of Battle Creek, pictured in this 1935 photograph. His original two inns were near downtown. This building, on the corner of West Michigan Avenue and Eldredge Street, was used as a stopover on the stagecoach route to Hastings and Richland. The site of many social events, it had a large room on the second floor for parties. The timber for the frame building was cut near Dowling at the Barney Saw Mill. The building at 1278 West Michigan Avenue is currently used for apartments. (Lower photograph courtesy Willard Library.)

The Urbandale Branch of the Peoples Savings and Loan opened on April 3, 1954, at 1375 West Michigan Avenue to serve the citizens of the west side of Battle Creek. One of many branch banks opening in the suburbs, it had a modern design with a large exterior clock and a drive-through window. Today, the building houses the International Brotherhood of Electrical Workers, Local 445 and continues to display a clock. (Upper photograph courtesy Willard Library.)

The Clark Equipment Company began its operations in Battle Creek in 1922. The forklift production at the Industrial Truck Division in Springfield boomed during World War II, and the company became a leading manufacturer of gasoline and battery-powered trucks and industrial towing tractors. The company's office complex stood on the west side of 24th Street near Lafayette Street. Pictured in the 1950s, the office building was demolished in the 1980s, leaving only the similarly designed factory on the east side of 24th Street, shown in the more recent photograph. (Lower photograph courtesy Willard Library.)

On November 18, 1881, the Case-Willard Thresher Manufacturing Company became the Advance Rumely Company, as shown in the *c.* 1900 photograph. Production in Battle Creek of the Advance thresher, invented by C. G. Case, ceased at the 170 Kendall Street factory in 1930. The Battle Creek City Garage opened its building in 2003 at a cost of $13 million. The garage stores and maintains city public works vehicles, buses, and police vehicles. (Upper photograph courtesy Frances Thornton Collection.)

Chapter 2
SCHOOLS

Battle Creek's first public school was a log structure located on East Michigan Avenue between the present W. K. Kellogg Foundation building and the foundation's parking structure. The logs were cut from the surrounding forest, but the interior floors and furniture were built from planks floated down the Battle Creek River from the sawmill in Bellevue. From that point until now, education has been an important part of the city's character. From day care to primary and secondary education and college degree programs, Battle Creek has welcomed private, parochial, and public teaching. Diverse educational opportunities serve a diverse population. This 1920s view, looking west from McCamly Street, shows Old No. 1, which opened on April 10, 1871, at a cost of $75,000. In 1910, the school became the city's first junior high, after the new high school was built facing Van Buren Street. The old school was demolished in 1934, after W. K. Kellogg Junior High School was built across the street. Today, the Battle Creek Central High School music building occupies the site. (Courtesy Willard Library.)

Battle Creek Central High School is pictured in three views looking northwest from the intersection of Van Buren and McCamly Streets. In 1909, the building was still under construction, with the observation dome not yet finished. The 1850s house on the corner was sold to the public school system and then demolished in 1927. Old No. 1 can be seen behind the high school here and in the 1920s view. The McQuiston Learning Center was constructed in 1978, and the high school complex was completely renovated in 2001 at a cost of nearly $8 million. (Upper photograph courtesy Frances Thornton Collection; middle photograph courtesy E. W. Roberts Collection of Willard Library.)

This 1930s photograph is of the Battle Creek Central High School athletic field on the northwest corner of West and Champion Streets. The land was acquired by the public schools in 1902 and was named Genebach Field after G. J. Genebach, the founder and president of United Steel and Wire. The Youth Building, the brick structure on Mykins Hill, was designed by the Grand Rapids architectural firm of Benjamin and Benjamin and was built in 1928. Upon completion, it was donated to the Associated Boys Clubs by W. K. Kellogg. In 1961, Marjorie Post May (C. W. Post's daughter) donated a quarter of a million dollars to completely renovate the field and stadium. The athletic facility is called C. W. Post Field. The Youth Building almost gave way to the wrecking ball but was spared and given new life as residential apartments called the Village at Irving Park. (Lower photograph courtesy E. W. Roberts Collection of Willard Library.)

McKinley Elementary School was designed by local architect A. D. Ordway and was built at 400 Capital Avenue Northeast in 1889. It was enlarged in 1901 and again in 1902. It is pictured in the 1930s in a view taken from across Union Street, looking northeast. The old building was demolished and a new building was constructed in the late 1970s. (Upper photograph courtesy E. W. Roberts Collection of Willard Library.)

In 1915, Verona School was constructed at a cost of $42,000. As shown in the 1920s photograph, half the building was erected next to the old 1894 wooden school. John Chubb was the architect. In 1929, the wooden structure was removed and a new $212,000 wing, designed by Chanel and Chute to match the other half, was added. The school housed junior high students as well as elementary grades until 1947, when the junior high was transferred to W. K. Kellogg Junior High School. (Lower photograph courtesy Frances Thornton Collection.)

In 1904, the area north of Emmett Street along North Avenue was dominated by a large man-made hill on the east side of the road, pictured from across North Avenue. Before the city decided on using the Verona Well Fields for its water supply, a local entrepreneur had attempted to build a reservoir by excavating the site, but the project had been abandoned, leaving a hill and a large crater. Kellogg Community College opened on the site in 1962 at a cost of $2 million. In 1965, the Miller Gymnasium-Pool was opened, followed by the Harry R. Davidson Visual and Performing Arts Building in 1971 and the Lyle C. Roll Health and Technology Center in 1979. The campus was extensively remodeled in the late 1990s. (Upper photograph courtesy Frances Thornton Collection.)

On September 19, 1921, Lakeview School opened at 300 Highland Avenue at a cost of $150,000. The building eventually became Lakeview High School and, later, Highland Junior High School. It was demolished in 1981, and the grocery store that replaced it used pieces of the old building to erect a marker commemorating the many students who had attended school there. (Lower photograph courtesy E. W. Roberts Collection of Willard Library.)

Spaulding School was built in 1868 at the southwest corner of Beckley and Beadle Lake Roads. Some 60 to 70 students attended the first year, with Mr. Hodges as their teacher. The upper photograph was taken in the early 1900s. The school was torn down in the 1950s as the Harper Creek School System's elementary-middle school and high school were constructed behind it. Built by Skanska Associates, the new Harper Creek High School was completed in 2004. (Upper photograph courtesy Willard Library.)

Chapter 3

Hospitals and Churches

Physical health and spiritual health are important to society. Battle Creek's first church services were held in private residences. Later, church members held services in the schoolhouse, and eventually, they built structures in which to practice their faith. Health care for the early pioneers was self-taught for most afflictions, unless the malady was serious enough to seek out a physician. Overall, the body and spirit of Battle Creek has kept up with the times. With new state-of-the-art medical facilities and all kinds of established churches thriving and new denominations starting, the city holistically has a clean bill of health. Pictured in the 1940s near the Emmett Street entrance is Leila Hospital, at 300 North Avenue. Leila Y. Post Montgomery, C. W. Post's widow, donated the hospital to the Sisters of Mercy to administer after having been a patient in a Mercy hospital in Detroit. The original 80-bed building (right) was formally dedicated on April 19, 1927. The 1929 addition (left) increased the bed count to 128. The hospital remained in use until the mid-1990s. (Courtesy Willard Library.)

The original 1926 section of Leila Hospital was still in use when the *c.* 1985 photograph was taken looking northwest from the Emmett Street entrance. The seven-story patient tower (left) was opened in 1970 as part of a citywide effort to improve and enlarge Battle Creek's four hospitals. The cancer care center (foreground) was opened in the 1980s. In 1988, the Community Hospital Association and Leila Hospital and Health Center combined to create Battle Creek Health System. All inpatient services were combined at the Leila site after the oldest part of the building was demolished to make way for the $70 million facility, with its new outpatient center (right).

On September 12, 1938, Community Hospital opened on West Street. Formerly known as Nichols Memorial Hospital, the institution moved from its Van Buren Street location near the Michigan Central Railroad tracks because of noise and smoke. The 1940s view is looking east from Brook Street over the Irving Park lagoon. Irving Park's lagoon was routed through underground pipes in the 1960s. Community Hospital was enlarged in the 1970s, and then it closed and combined with Leila Hospital, two blocks away, to become Battle Creek Health System in 1988. The old hospital building housed Southwest Michigan Rehab Services until 2005. A possible future use being discussed for the building is as an adult assisted-living facility. (Lower postcard courtesy Frances Thornton Collection.)

On February 18, 1902, the Battle Creek Sanitarium burned to the ground. A 550-foot-long, five-story sanitarium, designed by Dayton, Ohio, architect Frank M. Andrews, was dedicated on May 31, 1903. Pictured in the early 1900s, looking north from the intersection of Washington Avenue and Champion Street, the $1 million building was considered the "ideal hospital design."

The front entrance was flanked by open galleries, allowing patients plenty of fresh air and light, all important in Dr. John Harvey Kellogg's regimen of healthful living. The 15-story Towers addition was opened in 1928. The $3 million building contained 265 hotel-style guest rooms, furnished by Marshall Field and Company. The entire facility could accommodate 1,250 guests and 1,800 staff. In 1942, the building was sold to the federal government and became Percy Jones General Army Hospital, specializing in orthopedic surgery and treatments. It became the Federal Center in 1954, and it is currently known as the Hart, Dole and Inouye Federal Center. (Upper photograph courtesy Frances Thornton Collection.)

In 1901, Neil Phelps built a sanitarium on the west side of the Washington Avenue-West Emmett Street intersection, across from Dr. John Harvey Kellogg's Battle Creek Sanitarium. After Phelps's business failed, the Battle Creek Sanitarium acquired the building in 1911 and used it as an annex. In 1942, Kellogg sold the main sanitarium and moved all operations into the former Phelps building, the largest fieldstone building in North America. Later, the building became part of Battle Creek Health System. During demolition of the building in 1986, local historian and preservationist Duff Stoltz saved the cupola from the wrecking ball, and it is now the centerpiece for the Leila Arboretum Children's Garden at Leila Arboretum, on West Michigan Avenue, which opened in 2003.

Lakeview General Osteopathic Hospital was originally established in a house on Elm Street. On March 3, 1957, this building opened its doors to patients at 80 North 20th Street. Its 56 beds on two levels were served by a staff of 28 osteopathic physicians. The *c.* 1965 photograph shows a two-story addition under construction, which increased the bed count to 90. The hospital merged with Leila Hospital and Health Center in the 1980s, and the building was converted to an extended care facility called Mercy Pavilion. (Upper photograph courtesy Willard Library.)

The Roosevelt Community House, on Evergreen Road, was constructed at Camp Custer during World War I. On October 27, 1921, the building was turned over to the American Legion and became the American Legion Hospital. A tuberculosis wing was added in 1954 and used until 1961, after which it served as a general hospital. In the 1960s, the facility began specializing in long-term rehabilitation. It later evolved into Southwest Michigan Rehab Services. It is now vacant. (Lower photograph courtesy Willard Library.)

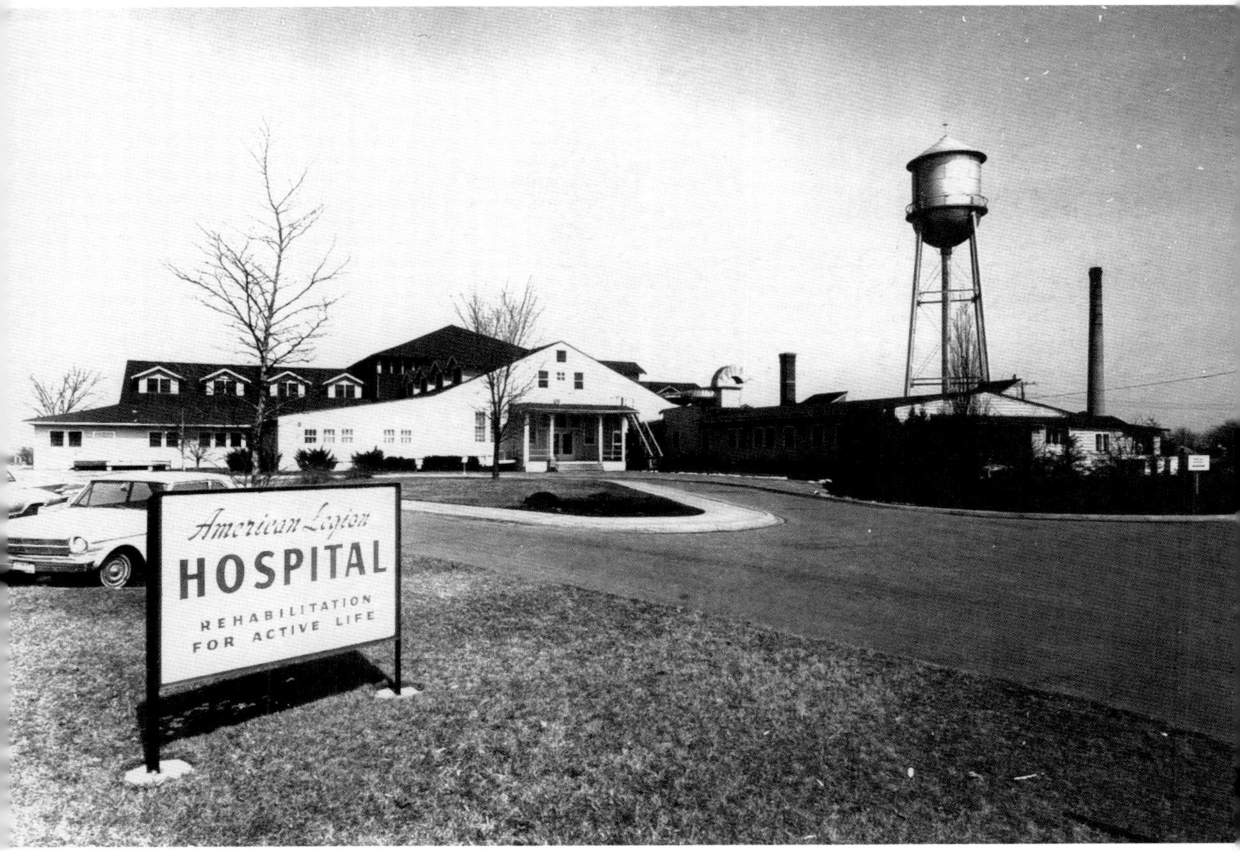

St. Philip Catholic Church, on the northeast corner of Van Buren Street and Maple Street (now Capital Avenue Northeast) was dedicated on November 27, 1879. The original building and its 1902 addition are shown in the earliest view. The 1914 addition is included in the middle view. The edifice burned in 1928, and the $200,000 Romanesque-style church, designed by Chanel and Chute, opened in 1930. (Upper and middle postcards courtesy Frances Thornton Collection; lower photograph courtesy E. W. Roberts Collection of Willard Library.)

The First Presbyterian Church, at 115 Capital Avenue Northeast, is pictured in the 1930s, with an empty lot on the left. The lot was once the site of the 1850 Colonial-style home of Rolden Kingman. The Kingman house was remodeled into a Christian Science church in 1908 and then demolished in 1931. The site was sold to George D. Farley, who built a $75,000 Colonial-themed funeral home, doing business today as Farley, Estes, Dowdle Funeral Service. (Lower photograph courtesy E. W. Roberts Collection of Willard Library.)

The First Congregational Church Building, at 145 Capital Avenue Northeast, was dedicated on October 11, 1908. The $80,000 edifice was designed by Chicago architect Joseph Llewellyn, who also designed Willard Library and Post School. Next to the church, in the 1930s photograph, is an 1845 house that served as the St. Thomas Episcopal Church rectory until it was purchased by the Congregational Church and demolished. The Congregational church parish house and offices were built in 1940. The Miller Chapel was dedicated in 1958. (Upper photograph courtesy E. W. Roberts Collection of Willard Library.)

The Maple Methodist Church, on the southeast corner of Maple Street (now Capital Avenue Northeast) and Merritt Street, was dedicated on August 31, 1890. It derived its name from its location on Maple Street. In 1903, a 12-room parsonage was built on the south side of the church, and in 1920, another addition containing a gymnasium was completed, as shown in the 1920s photograph. The parsonage was demolished for the 1974 education wing. (Lower photograph courtesy Martin Ashley Collection.)

The 1940s view of downtown Battle Creek shows, from left to right, the Milner Hotel (formerly the Williams House), the Michigan National Bank Building, the Old Merchants National Bank (now Heritage Tower), the Battle Creek Sanitarium Building (now the Hart, Dole and Inouye Federal Center), the Central National Bank (now the Battle Creek Tower), and stores that are on the present site of the W. K. Kellogg Foundation. Becoming part of this visual history, authors Kurt Thornton (left) and Martin Ashley (right) hope that you have enjoyed looking at the city and have perhaps gained a little better understanding of where it all came from. Their final words are, "Remember, we are all history." (Upper photograph courtesy of Willard Library.)